Suzuki®

STRING ORCHESTRA ACCOMPANIMENTS

to Solos From Suzuki® Violin School

Volumes 1 & 2

Arranged by Paul Schwartz
Selected and Edited by John Kendall

CONTENTS

© 1955, 1970 Dr. Shinichi Suzuki
Sole publisher for the entire world except Japan:
Summy-Birchard, Inc.
Exclusive print rights administered by Alfred Music Publishing Co., Inc.
All rights reserved   Printed in USA

ISBN-10: 0-87487-318-5
ISBN-13: 978-0-87487-318-4

The Suzuki name, logo and wheel device
are trademarks of Dr. Shinichi Suzuki
used under exclusive license by Summy-Birchard, Inc.

Preface

These orchestrations are designed to serve as accompaniments for the solos in Volumes 1 and 2 of the Suzuki repertory. While they are complete in themselves, the piano accompaniment or the second violin part in Suzuki's *Duets for Two Violins* may be used in conjunction with them.

The texture has been kept light in order to avoid covering an individual soloist or a small group. It should be kept in mind, however, that a group of fifty or more soloists, even with small violins, will cover a full string orchestra, and a piano may be needed for extra support in those circumstances.

The arrangements have been kept at a technical level available to junior high orchestras but will of course be effective for more advanced players as well.

Bowings agree with the solo parts, except for occasional departures to improve orchestral sound. Fingerings have been left to the players, except for a few suggested positions in the cello part. Bass parts are optional but will add to the sonority.

There have been some omissions from the complete repertory, either because the accompaniment is so intrinsically pianistic (i.e., "The Two Grenadiers") or because certain compositions seem more effective than others in group performance.

It is hoped that these string accompaniments, along with the already existing orchestrations for some of the standard repertory, will provide an added musical experience for young violinists.

JOHN KENDALL

Twinkle, Twinkle, Little Star Variations

Shinichi Suzuki

Lightly Row

Song of the Wind

Folk Song

Go Tell Aunt Rhody

O Come, Little Children

May Song

Allegro

Shinichi Suzuki

Long, Long Ago

T. H. Bayly

9
f
mf
mf
mf
mf
mp
p
p
p
p
13
poco rit.
f
mf
mf
mf
mf

The Happy Farmer

15
mf
p
p
f
mf
f
mf
f
mf
mf
f
f

Chorus from "Judas Maccabeus"

G. F. Handel

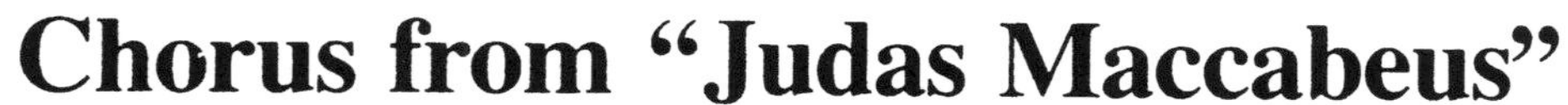

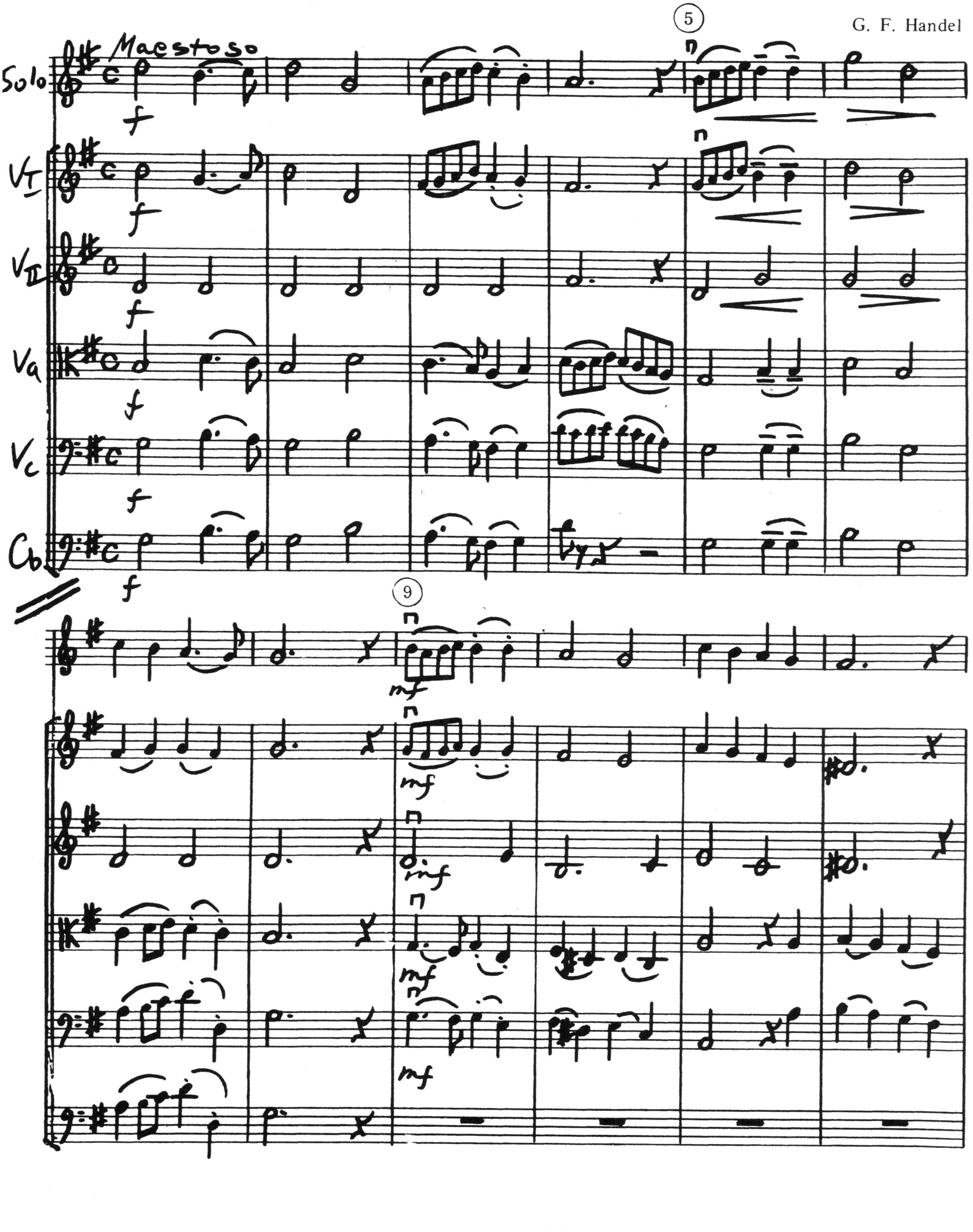

13
rall.
17
f
21
rall.
f

Perpetual Motion

Shinichi Suzuki

9
13
p
p
p
p
p
p

pizz.
f
f

Hunters' Chorus

C. M. von Weber

15
21
pizz.
arco
pizz.
arco
pizz.
arco
pizz.
arco
pizz.
arco

Theme from "Witches' Dance"

N. Paganini

25 Meno mosso
p
Meno mosso
p pizz.
Meno mosso
p pizz.
Meno mosso
p pizz.
Meno mosso
p pizz.
Meno mosso
p pizz.
3
3
arco
arco
arco
arco
arco

32 a tempo
f a tempo
f a tempo
f a tempo
f a tempo
f a tempo
f
37

Gavotte

Allegretto
mf con grazia
Solo
V I
V II
Va
Vc
Cb
mp
mp
mp
mp
pizz.
mp
5
9
J. B. Lully

13
tr.
Rit.
a tempo
Rit.
a tempo
Rit.
a tempo
Rit.
a tempo
Rit.
a tempo

22
FINE
rall.
rall.
rall.
rall.
rall.
rall.
26

31
rit. D.C. al FINE
rit. D.C. al FINE
rit. D.C. al FINE
rit. D.C. al FINE
rit. D.C. al FINE
arco

Bourrée

G. F. Handel
Solo
Allegretto
p
espr.
V I
p
V II
p
Va
p
Vc
p
Cb
p
5
cresc.
mf
p
f
cresc.
mf
p
mf
cresc.
mf
p
mf
cresc.
mf
p
mf
cresc.
mf
p
mf
cresc.
mf
p
1.
2.

9
dim.
dim.
dim.
dim.
dim.
mf
dim.
13

17
21
(2nd time: Rit.)
1.
2.
cresc.
ff
f
f
cresc.
f
mf
cresc.
f
mf
cresc.
f
mf
cresc.
f
mf
cresc.
f
mf